HOW TO DRAW
THE HUMAN FIGURE

Mark Bergin

BOOK HOUSE

SALARIYA

© The Salariya Book Company Ltd MMIX

Published in Great Britain in MMIX by
Book House, an imprint of
The Salariya Book Company Ltd
25 Marlborough Place, Brighton BN1 1UB

3 5 7 9 8 6 4 2

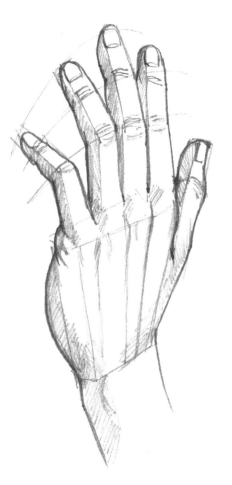

Please visit our website at **www.salariya.com**
for **free** electronic versions of:
You Wouldn't Want to Be an Egyptian Mummy!
You Wouldn't Want to Be a Roman Gladiator!
Avoid Joining Shackleton's Polar Expedition!
Avoid Sailing on a 19th-Century Whaling Ship!

Author: Mark Bergin was born in Hastings in 1961. He studied at Eastbourne College of Art and has specialised in historical reconstructions as well as aviation and maritime subjects since 1983. He lives in Bexhill-on-Sea with his wife and three children.

Editor: Rob Walker

PB ISBN: 978-1-906714-51-2

A CIP catalogue record for this book is available from the British Library.

Printed and bound in China.
Printed on paper from
sustainable sources.
Reprinted in 2009.

WARNING: Fixatives should be used only under adult supervision.

PAPER FROM
SUSTAINABLE
FORESTS

Contents

Making a start

Learning to draw is about looking and seeing. Keep practising, and get to know your subject. Use a sketchbook to make quick drawings. Start by doodling, and experiment with shapes and patterns. There are many ways to draw; this book shows only some methods. Visit art galleries, look at artists' drawings, see how friends draw, but above all, find your own way.

You can practise drawing figures using an artist's wooden model to try out various poses.

When drawing from photos, use construction lines to help you to understand the form of the body and the relationship between each of its parts.

4

Sketch people in everyday surroundings. This will help you to draw faster to capture the main elements of a pose quickly.

Try sketching friends and family at home.

You can create new poses by drawing simple stick figures.

Figure proportions

This page shows the standard proportions of a human figure. Normally the length of a human head will fit seven or eight times into its body height.

The proportions of a male figure shown from different views.

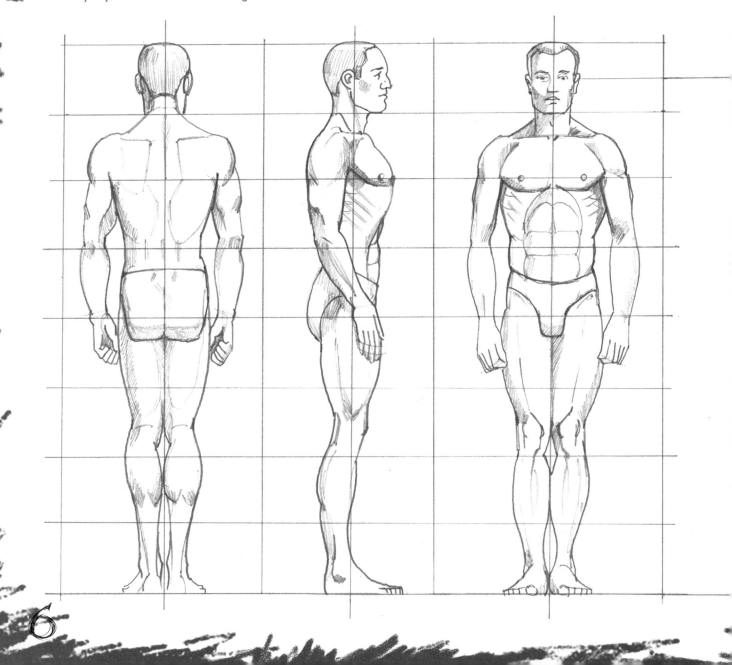

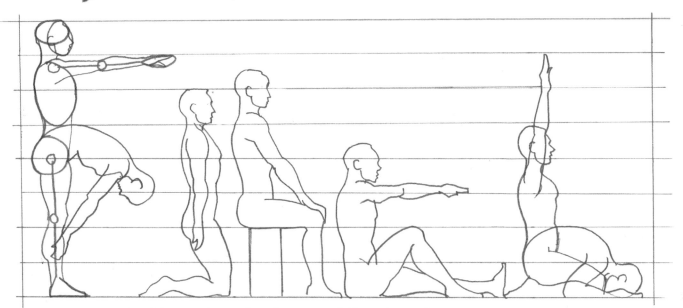

This shows the height variation of a figure in different positions.

The proportions of a female figure shown from different views.

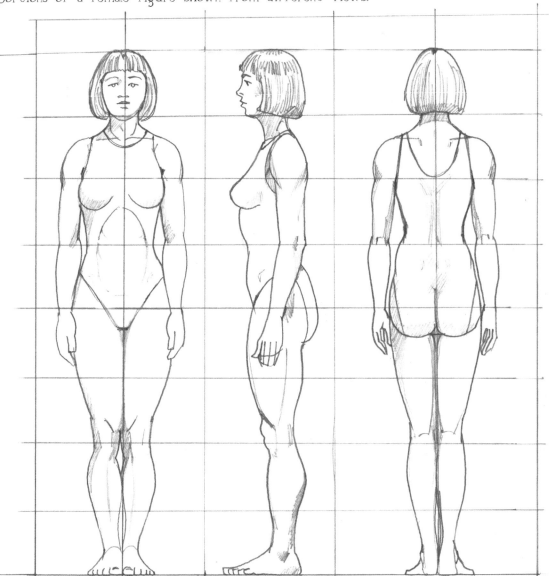

7

Perspective

If you look at a figure from different viewpoints, you will see that whichever part is closest to you looks larger, and the part furthest away from you looks smallest. Drawing in perspective is a way of creating a feeling of depth — of suggesting three dimensions on a flat surface.

V.P.

V.P.

The vanishing point (V.P.) is the place in a perspective drawing where parallel lines appear to meet. The position of the vanishing point depends on the viewer's eye level.

Two-point perspective drawing

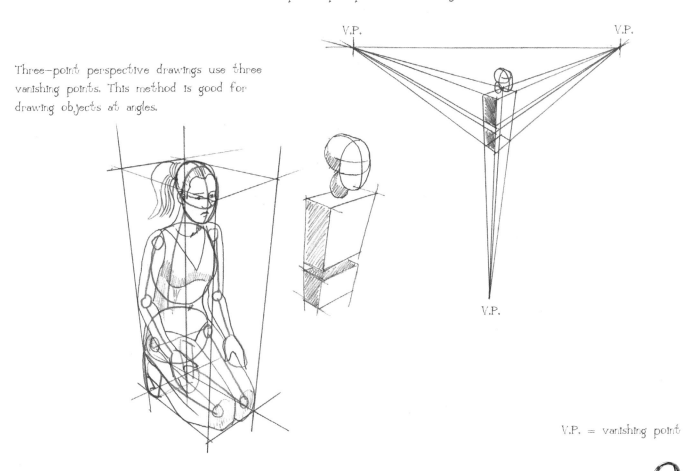

Two-point perspective uses two vanishing points: one for lines running along the length of the object, and another on the opposite side for lines running across the width of the object.

V.P.   V.P.

Once you have the basic components of the body, move on to drawing in the stick-figure skeleton. From here you can draw the shape of the body.

Three-point perspective drawing

Three-point perspective drawings use three vanishing points. This method is good for drawing objects at angles.

V.P.   V.P.

V.P.

V.P. = vanishing point

9

Drawing materials

Try using different types of drawing papers and materials. Experiment with charcoal, wax crayons and pastels. All pens, from felt-tips to ballpoints, will make interesting marks — or try drawing with pen and ink on wet paper.

Pencil

Felt-tip

Hard **pencils** are greyer and soft pencils are blacker. Hard pencils are graded from 6H (the hardest) through 5H, 4H, 3H and 2H to H. Soft pencils are graded from B, 2B, 3B, 4B and 5B up to 6B (the softest).

Charcoal is very soft and can be used for big, bold drawings. Ask an adult to spray your charcoal drawings with fixative to prevent smudging.

Pastels are even softer than charcoal, and come in a wide range of colours. Ask an adult to spray your pastel drawings with fixative to prevent smudging.

You can create special effects by scraping away parts of a drawing done with **wax crayons**.

Silhouette is a style of drawing that uses only a solid black shadow.

Pen and ink

Pastels

Lines drawn in ink cannot be erased, so keep your ink drawings sketchy and less rigid. Don't worry about mistakes as these lines can be lost in the drawing as it develops.

11

The muscles

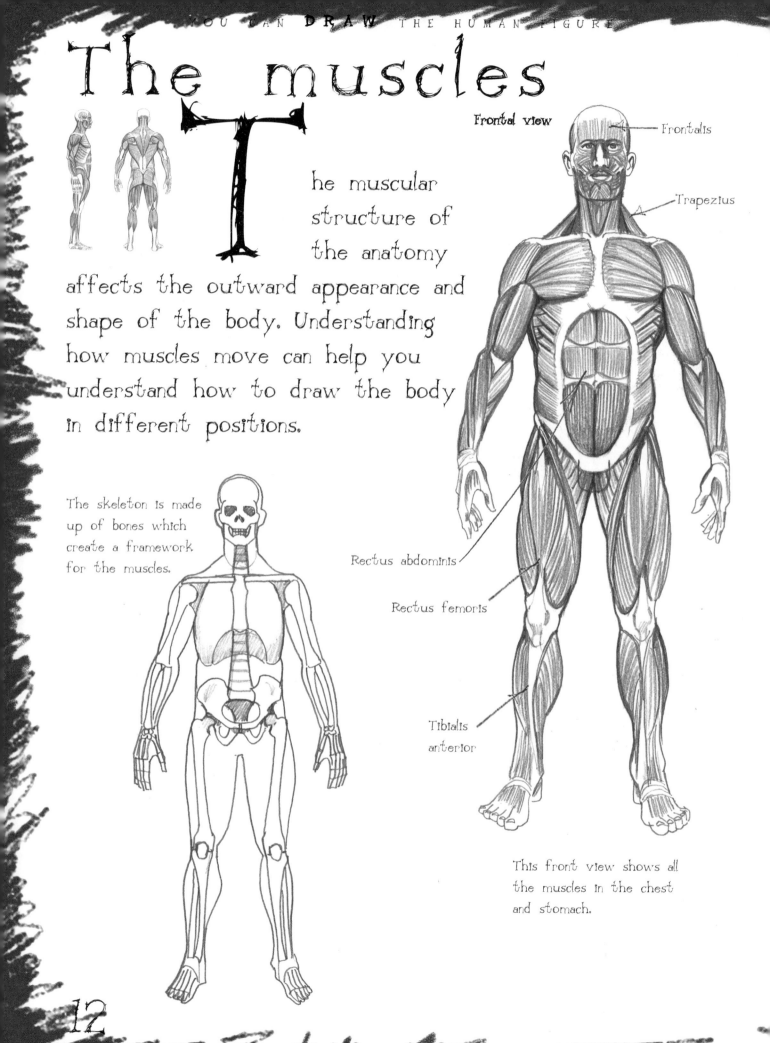

The muscular structure of the anatomy affects the outward appearance and shape of the body. Understanding how muscles move can help you understand how to draw the body in different positions.

Frontal view

Frontalis

Trapezius

Rectus abdominis

Rectus femoris

Tibialis anterior

The skeleton is made up of bones which create a framework for the muscles.

This front view shows all the muscles in the chest and stomach.

12

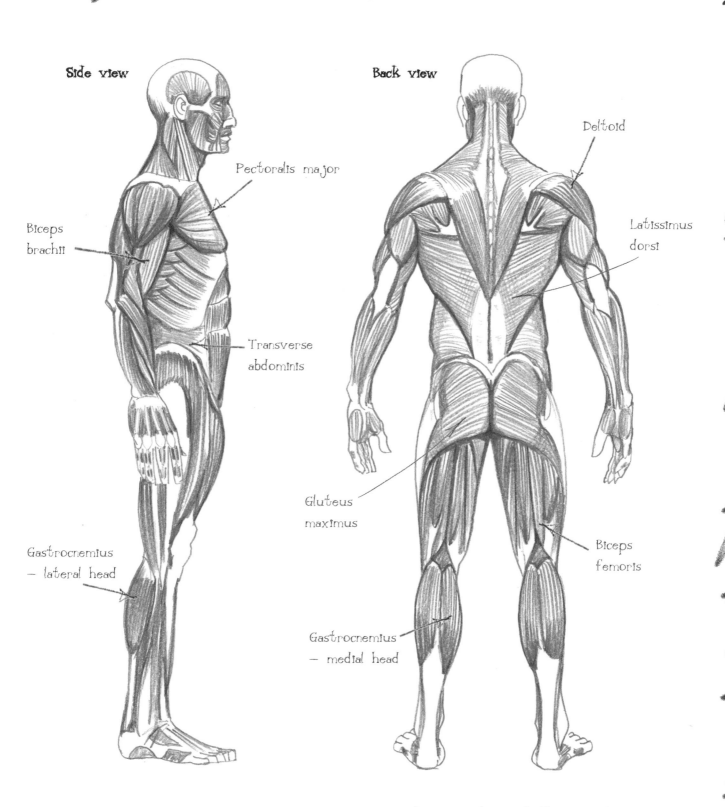

Side view

Pectoralis major

Biceps
brachii

Transverse
abdominis

Gastrocnemius
— lateral head

Back view

Deltoid

Latissimus
dorsi

Gluteus
maximus

Biceps
femoris

Gastrocnemius
— medial head

This view shows all the muscular
structure from the side.

This view shows all the muscular
structure from the back.

The head

T he head is a difficult shape to draw. It includes some of the most expressive features of the body. Using construction lines helps to place the eyes, nose, ears and mouth accurately on the head.

Frontal view

Squaring up the paper can help you to decide the positions of the facial features

Draw the main shape of the head by overlapping two ovals.

When drawing the head from different angles, construction lines can help to keep the features in the correct positions.

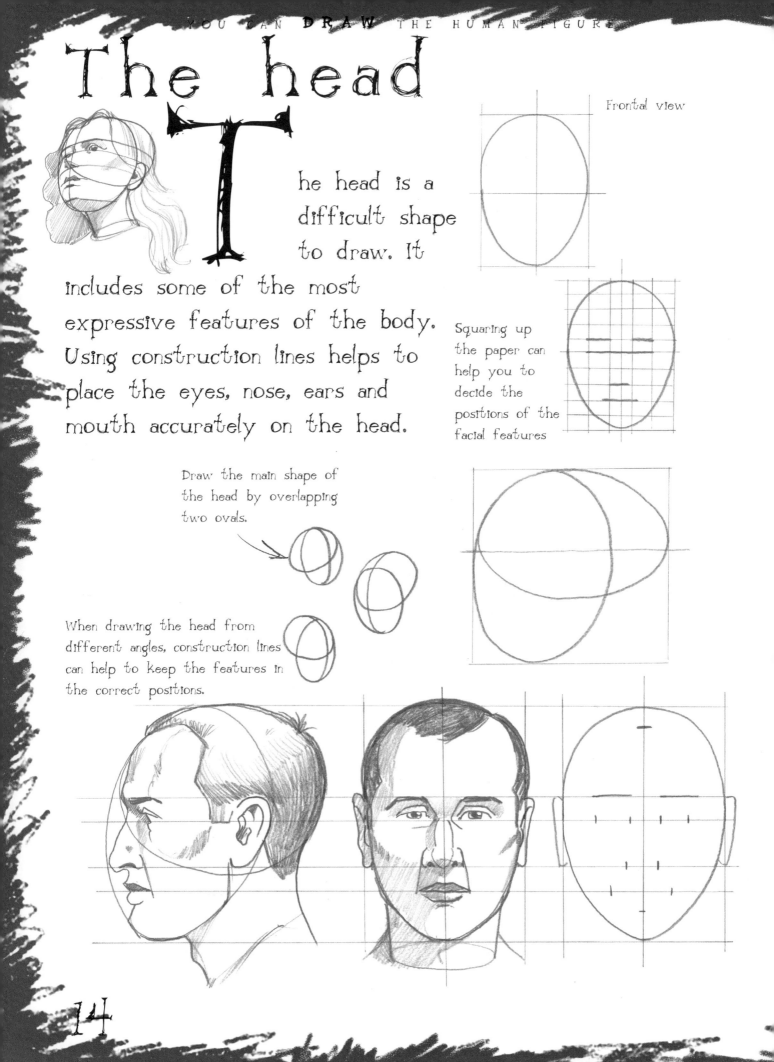

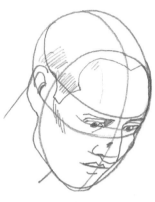

Draw in construction lines to show where each facial feature begins and ends.

These construction lines have been used to draw a male head.

These construction lines have been used to draw a female head.

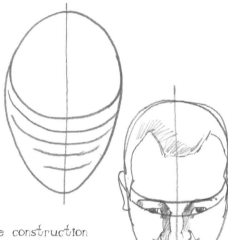

Add detail and any extra features such as hair.

These construction lines show the head facing downwards.

The curved construction lines help you to place the features.

These construction lines show a head facing upwards.

Draw in the feature. Do not forget the underside of the chin.

Complete any details and remove unwanted construction lines.

15

Ears, nose and mouth

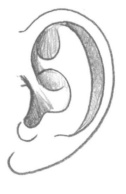

The basic shape of an ear is made with several curved lines.

The ears, nose and mouth are important features of the head. See how they are constructed and how they look viewed from different angles.

Add tone to create the three-dimensional structure of the ear.

Use construction lines and perspective to help draw ears from different angles.

Ears can be many different shapes and sizes; however, their construction is essentially the same.

Always check your light source to see how it affects areas of light and dark in your drawing.

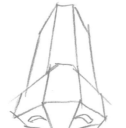

The nose is formed using these basic shapes.

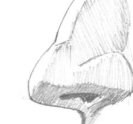

Noses can be many different shapes and sizes.

Viewed from below, the nostril cavities need heavy shading.

Viewed from above, the nostrils cannot be seen.

This view captures almost all of the features of the nose.

The mouth is formed using these basic shapes. Add tone and shade to define the lips.

The side view of the mouth is formed by a triangular shape using curved lines.

Viewed from below, the mouth is curved downwards at each side.

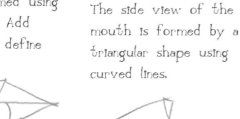

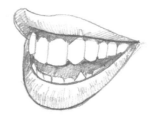

To draw an open mouth, leave areas of white for the teeth. Add some shading under the top lip.

A wide-open mouth shows the tongue.

A smiling mouth is much wider and shows more teeth.

17

The eyes

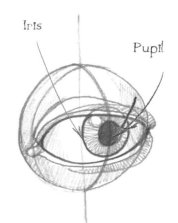

Iris

Pupil

Each eyeball sits in a socket in the head. It is surrounded by the protective eyelids. The eyes and eyebrows are very expressive.

The eyeball is spherical in shape. Its most visible features are the iris and pupil. Start by drawing a spherical eyeball. Add the shape of the eyelids.

Male eye

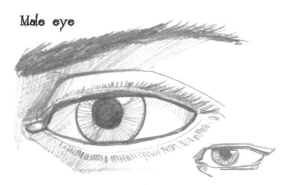

Once the visible part of the eye is drawn add detail to the iris. Leave an area of white for a highlight.

Female eye

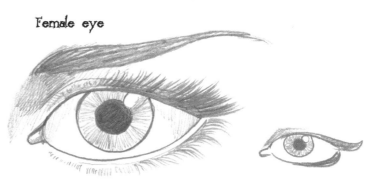

Consider details around the eye; the length of the eyelashes and the eyebrow shape.

When drawing the eye from the side it is important to use perspective.

Check your light source before adding tone to the drawing. Darker areas tend to be where the nose projects out from the eyes.

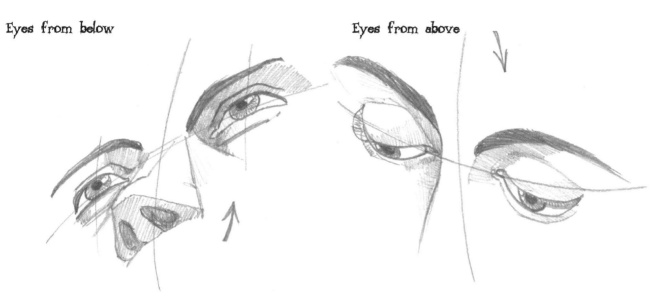

Eyes from below

Eyes from above

When drawing the eyes from this angle, use a downward-curved construction line to place them accurately.

Drawing the eyes from above means you see less of the eyeball.

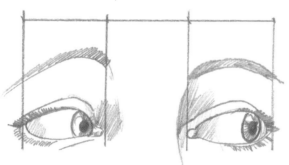

When drawing both eyes it is very important that they relate correctly in scale. It helps to start your drawing using carefully worked out construction lines.

With this view it is important to consider the light source.

Partially shut eyelids show less of the eyeball. Add more shaded areas.

The position of the pupil and iris is important as it shows where the eyes are looking. Keep their direction similar.

19

The hands

The hand is one of the most complex parts of a figure to draw. It consists of many moving parts, and therefore can be drawn in a huge variety of poses.

The hand can be broken down into basic shapes and areas.

Each finger has three sections, a thumb has two sections, and the main area of the hand has three.

Sketch in these shapes as three-dimensional boxes. Construction lines can then be drawn for a variety of poses.

Using the construction lines as a guide you can draw the hand. Add tone and detail to finish off.

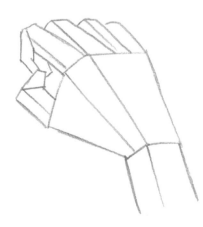

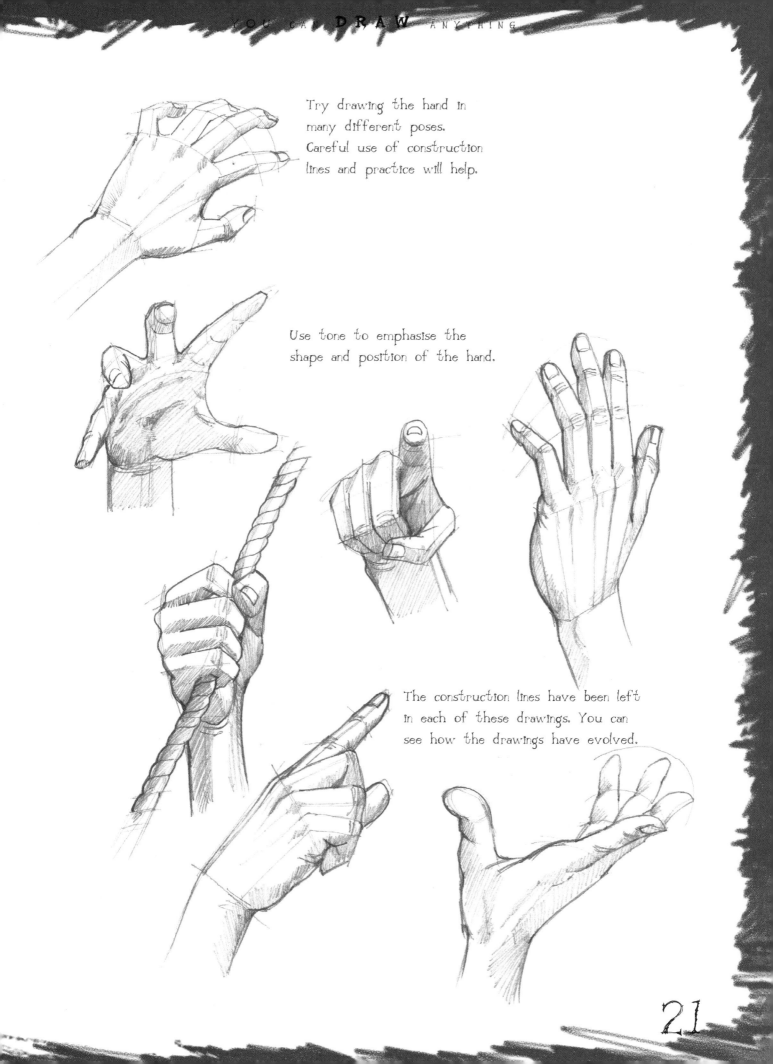

Try drawing the hand in many different poses. Careful use of construction lines and practice will help.

Use tone to emphasise the shape and position of the hand.

The construction lines have been left in each of these drawings. You can see how the drawings have evolved.

The Feet

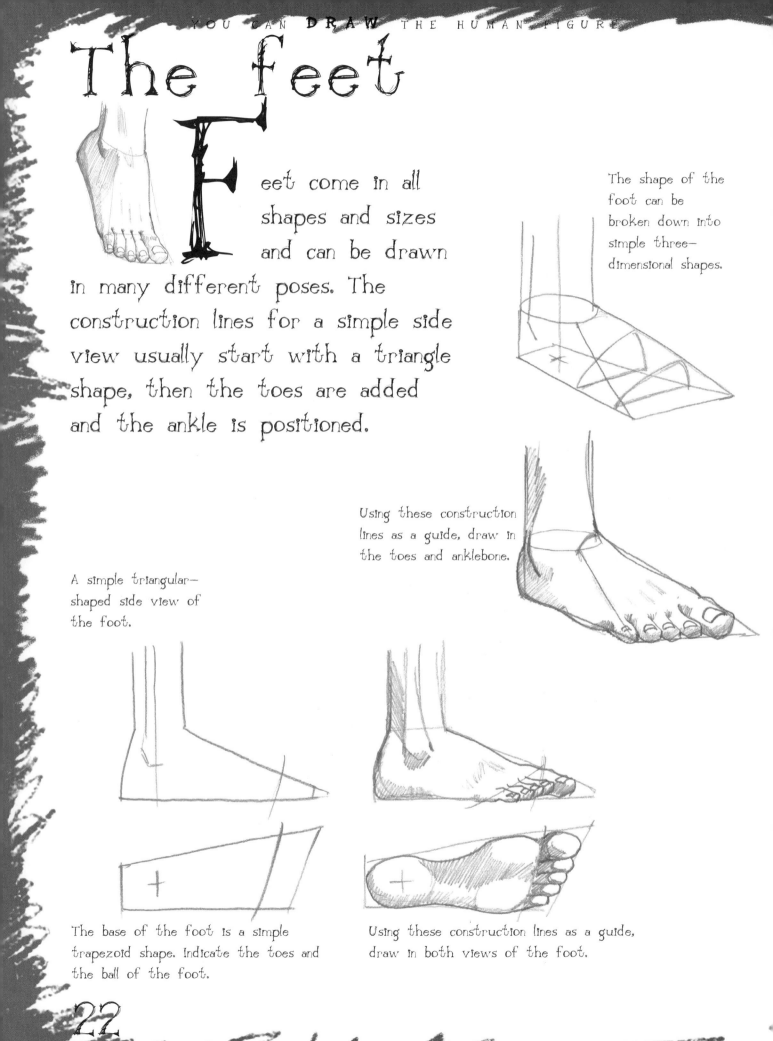

Feet come in all shapes and sizes and can be drawn in many different poses. The construction lines for a simple side view usually start with a triangle shape, then the toes are added and the ankle is positioned.

The shape of the foot can be broken down into simple three-dimensional shapes.

Using these construction lines as a guide, draw in the toes and anklebone.

A simple triangular-shaped side view of the foot.

The base of the foot is a simple trapezoid shape. Indicate the toes and the ball of the foot.

Using these construction lines as a guide, draw in both views of the foot.

22

This page shows the foot drawn in
a variety of different poses. The
construction lines have been left in
to show how the shape and position
of the foot have evolved.

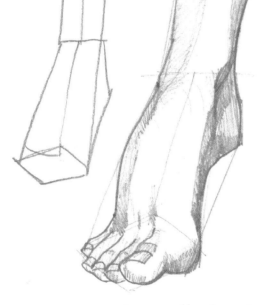

Draw in the toes. Position them within
the area of the construction lines.

Add tone to your drawing to indicate
the direction of the light source.

23

Standing figure

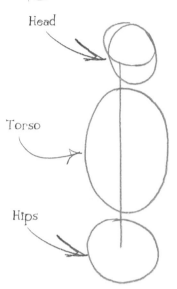

A standing figure can be drawn using a simple framework of construction lines. This basic starting point is a very good way to establish the correct proportions of a human figure in your drawing. The standing figure is a surfer holding his board.

Head

Torso

Hips

Start by drawing in a large oval between two circles for the head, torso and hips; Add a centre line.

Add two small circles for the shoulders either side of the large oval.

Draw in both arms using straight lines. Indicate the elbow joints using straight lines.

Draw two small circles either side of the hips; this will be the top of the legs. Draw a horizontal line to join the circles.

Add ovals to each arm for the hands

Add triangles to show the shape and direction of the feet.

Add straight lines for both legs. Indicate the knee joints with small circles.

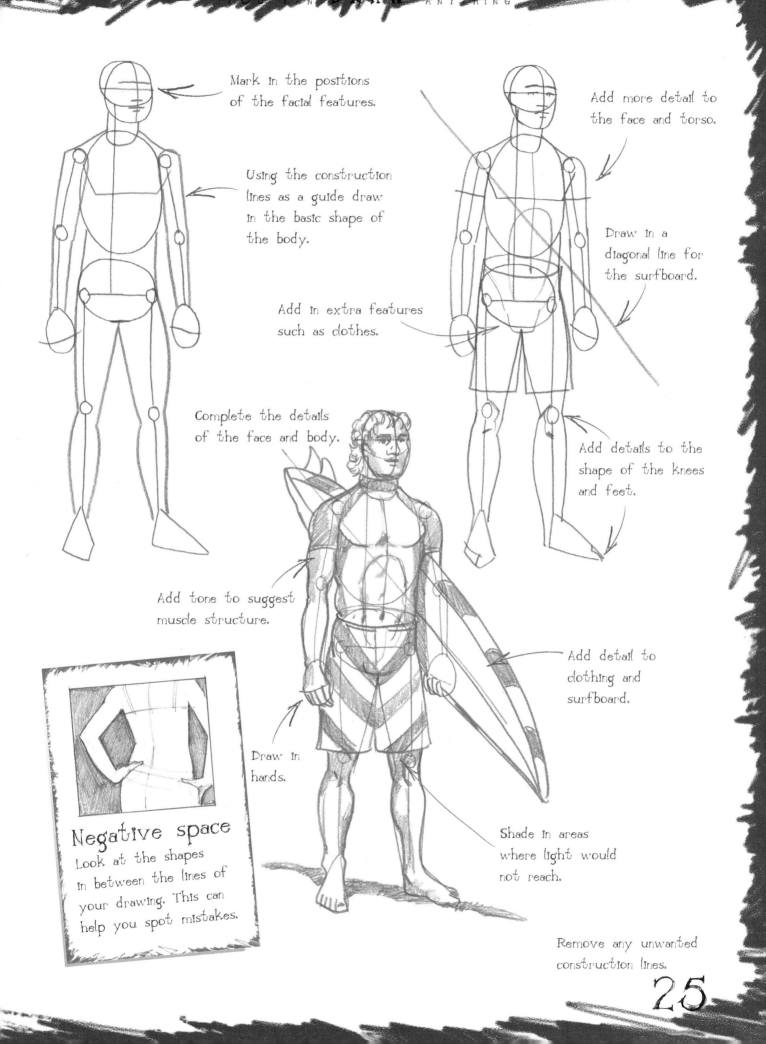

Mark in the positions of the facial features.

Using the construction lines as a guide draw in the basic shape of the body.

Add more detail to the face and torso.

Draw in a diagonal line for the surfboard.

Add in extra features such as clothes.

Complete the details of the face and body.

Add details to the shape of the knees and feet.

Add tone to suggest muscle structure.

Add detail to clothing and surfboard.

Draw in hands.

Shade in areas where light would not reach.

Negative space

Look at the shapes in between the lines of your drawing. This can help you spot mistakes.

Remove any unwanted construction lines.

25

Balance and motion

Motion and balance are important aspects to consider in your drawing. Use basic construction lines to create a variety of poses. Then build up the drawing from there.

A ballet dancer is a perfect example to show balance in the human body.

Draw in the position of the head and body using construction lines (as shown in previous pages). Pay particular attention to the curve and direction of the spine and hips.

Add the limbs; indicate the elbow and knee joints with small circles between straight lines. Draw in the hand positions using ovals and draw triangles for each foot.

Using construction lines draw a simple stick figure either running or walking. Study people as they walk by to see how their body moves.

A tennis player. Note the changes in balance as the racket is swung.

This figure is performing a long jump. The red line shows the flow of the hands through each stage of the jump.

When the basic structure of the figure is complete, start building up the shape of the body.

Keep the drawing quite light and sketchy at first until you are confident that the proportions are right.

Then begin to add tone and detail to finish the drawing. Remember to remove any unwanted construction lines.

Walking figure

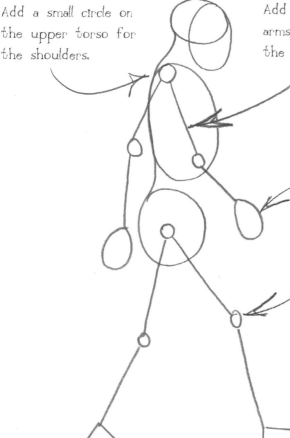

A simple walking movement is a good starting point for drawing a figure in motion. In this case the figure is viewed from the side, so remember to consider which parts of the body will be seen.

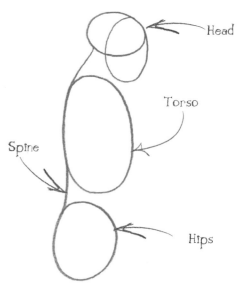

Head

Torso

Spine

Hips

Draw in the basic shapes for the head, torso and hips. Join these shapes with a line for the spine.

Add a small circle on the upper torso for the shoulders.

Add straight lines for the arms with small circles at the elbow joints.

Draw ovals to indicate the hands.

Draw a small circle in the middle of the hips. This indicates the top of each leg. Add straight lines for the legs with small circles for the knee joints.

Add in a basic triangular shape for each foot.

Using the construction lines as a guide, start to add the shape of the body.

Pay particular attention to the joints of each limb, drawing elbows and knees accordingly.

Use curved lines for the shape of the body.

Mirror

You can often see mistakes in a drawing by looking at it in reverse in a mirror.

Start to add in the facial features.

Add in muscle structure.

Complete the details of the facial features and hair.

Using the ovals as a guide, add detail to the hands.

Add clothing to the figure.

Add tone for definition.

Add muscles to the legs using the joints as a guide.

Add shoes.

Add shade to areas where light will not reach.

Add socks.

Remove any unwanted construction lines.

Running figure

A running figure makes a dynamic and powerful action pose. Study the shapes made by someone running and then draw the basic structure. Try to get a strong sense of movement to give life to your drawing.

Draw in the basic shapes for the head, torso and hips. Add a line for the spine.

Add a small circle either side of the upper torso to mark the shoulders.

Draw in the arms using straight lines with small circles to indicate the elbow joints.

Add ovals to position the hands.

Draw in the legs using straight lines with small circles for the knee joints.

Add in a basic triangular shape for each foot.

Each limb is bent at the joint.

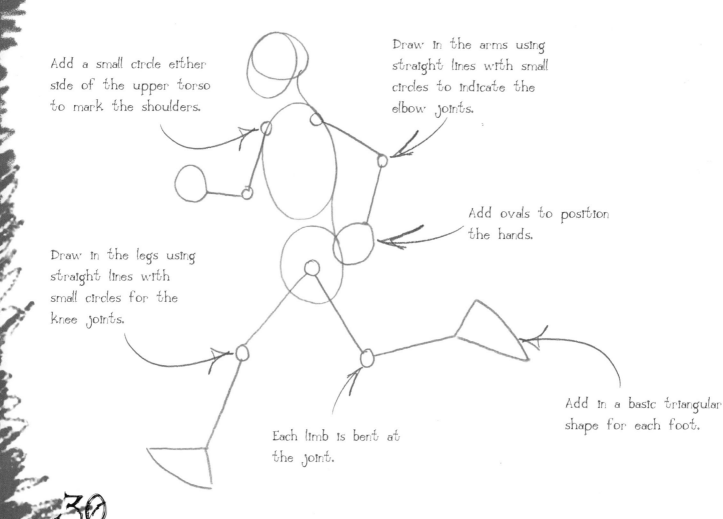

30

Add facial features to the head.

Sketch in the shape of the body. Use curved lines for arms and legs.

Proportions

Hold a pencil out at arm's length. Use it to help measure the proportions of the figure.

Add detail to the hands.

Draw in the shape of the trainers.

Complete the details of the facial features and the hair.

Add tone to define the muscles.

Add muscle to the arms and legs.

Draw in the clenched fists.

Add in clothing, making sure it fits around the body.

Add the detail of the trainers.

Add shade to areas where light would not reach.

Remove any unwanted construction lines.

31

Glossary

Centre line Often used as the starting point of the drawing, it marks the middle of the object or figure.

Composition The arrangement of the parts of a picture on the drawing paper.

Construction lines Guidelines used in the early stages of a drawing, and usually erased later.

Fixative A type of resin used to spray over a finished drawing to prevent smudging. **It should only be used by an adult.**

Light source The direction from which the light seems to come in a drawing.

Perspective A method of drawing in which near objects are shown larger than faraway objects to give an impression of depth.

Pose The position assumed by a figure.

Proportion The correct relationship of scale between each part of the drawing.

Silhouette A drawing that shows only a flat dark shape, like a shadow.

Vanishing point The place in a perspective drawing where parallel lines appear to meet.

Index